SURVIVAL CRESCENDO Cynical PANG
Questions Boston Illinois FRUIT
SHEPHERD Repentance AMNESTY Logic
German ANCHORED ROOT
Six CrookedLead we Jef
BE DANCE Seoul POWDER Harris
Sonorant Monophonic TARGETS

First poem of words

SPIRIT Viscous SING VESSELS Children
Ataraxia BEAUTY TREATS
MUSICIAN Mask Confronts Moon BARITONE
ARMS peeled
New Jersey Justice Rejoice
SPRING Luxembourg JOY Armor
Flesh Conviction God Chicago BOY VENDACE
Whispers Wrecking
Subdued REJECTION Swatter
Massachusetts Penetrant SOUL
Power AMERICA Home Sweetness French
SUMMER FLAG STOMACH BROWN
Meaningful Bummer Love Fall Sword
Hope Kaiserslautern Forgive
Surprises Korean Savor Paris Mercy
Golden PASSION Praying SATISFIED

Order this book online at www.trafford.com
or email orders@trafford.com

Most Trafford titles are also available at major online book retailers.

Printed in the United States of America.

ISBN: 978-1-4669-1034-8 (sc)
ISBN: 978-1-4669-1035-5 (hc)
ISBN: 978-1-4669-1036-2 (e)

Library of Congress Control Number: 2011963567

Trafford rev. 08/06/2012

 www.trafford.com

North America & international
toll-free: 1 888 232 4444 (USA & Canada)
phone: 250 383 6864 ♦ fax: 812 355 4082

Contents

Unknown

Author's Note

There are no substitutions for the words that found their way into this collection. This is what I want to say. I'm asking for consideration, appreciation, and understanding.

The three unrelated words that divide sections of this book are not intended to name chapters, since there are only two chapters: Poetry and Lyrics. They represent an exercise I call "TriWords". I use them as a pause. Examine their structure and movement. Speak them out loud. Look them up.

Yes, meaning is important but I didn't consider conventional denotations when choosing my TriWords, only their linguistic allure. Have fun and enjoy the words.

Jef, November 2011

Integrity

Cogent

Justice

Jef Harris

Paris 1980

The street was too narrow
The bus was too big and
You parked like a toddler.

The driver couldn't back
Us out of that crooked
Lane. He had to go forward.

It took four of us
To pick up your Renault
And sit it on the sidewalk.

I'm sure you must have
Been shocked mute when
You saw your car up four

And over eighteen inches.
Sorry, we didn't leave
You a note. You wouldn't

Have liked our reprimand
For lousy parking and
Inconsideration. Besides,

We couldn't write it in
French, then. C'est la vie![1]
Sommes-nous pardoner?[2]

---

[1]   That's life!
[2]   Are we forgiven?

Yearbook, 1968

As a Teen

I knew much about music and theory, nothing about musicianship.
This lesson came later, hard; tombstone against skull hard!

From second chair baritone, I stole piccolo and clarinet parts,
Oboe and flute solos. No woodwind was off limits, only brass.

The phrases sounded offensively diverse on my horn.
I thought I was cute, amusing, and versatile.

Playing during the bandmaster's instructions was normal.
Horn parts were boring; unchallenging for the caliber of musician
I thought I was.

I infuriated him so much he vehemently ordered me out of the
band room
And to report to the office. I was surprised it wasn't permanent.

I got ejected for other amateur pranks: blaring, not following
The music, playing impulsively, or not at all.

Once a couple of band mates joined me in protest when I was
expelled.
See, someone signified on a tuba player and it was riotous;
everyone laughed,

But I laughed the longest, and the loudest. For that I was told to
leave the class
And the bassoonist, a trumpet player, and saxophonist walked
with me.

One day the bandmaster introduced some new music with some
tough
Baritone parts; that's when my pompous performances ended.

I would like to say that when I graduated, I apologized to the
bandmaster
And my band mates for my clown tactics during all those
practices: I didn't.

Mates and Master, I'm sorry for the frustrations and disruptions to
your learning
I caused. Please forgive me. Master, I am humbled by your letting
me stay in the band.

you killed the beauty

you killed the beauty that laid me down
beneath a pale half-moon
long brown hair tickled my ears
as you pecked softly at my face
lips soft and warm

you killed the beauty those pearl white teeth
that blinded when you smiled
made me lie
about me
what I was feeling
to steal that first kiss

you killed the beauty that made you you
tender with compassion
bold with your love
effective in communication
honest with answers
firm with mistakes
especially in your friends

you killed the beauty that made me pilfer
from my songwriting
time and attention
to cover you in detail
searching for the reasons
why the beauty died
somewhere between
the powder the needle and the need

Temptation and Repentance

I think about you . . .
Manners, in which I should not.
Difficult to stop.

Spirit confronts flesh
You are sister not lover.
Jesus, forgive me!

Fragments of a Nightmare

A deaf horse rode a man up a hill of dead waiters.
Foaming at the mouth, the man tripped over a tray

Of Wheat Thins and Edam cheese, fell, and broke his leg.
The horse tore off his other leg and beat him into

A watery pulp that oozed down the hill to a weeping widow.
My dead brother, executed for running a red light, begs

For leniency on account of his thirst to be first
While my dead sister pleads through giggles

As she pens his poetic eulogy with flawed pathetic fallacy.
Seven fevered pallid children riding three-legged dogs,

Shooting pregnant Chinese girls in their stomachs with blue lasers.
Meanwhile, I'm sitting Arapaho-style on the edge of an active
volcano,

Holding a fifth of Chivas Regal in my lap, polishing my eyeballs,
And eating my pancreas while using my pain to attract a crowd of
sobbing saints.

first poem of words

amnesty arid broidery bell
lagan misty fawn
magical <u>vendace</u> tapestry fell
dangling dizzy dawn

jewelry jetsam silvery foam
gamy frosty fur
circular city radiance roam
smothering sinter sur

sonorant supor pastoral sone
raspy rosy fade
petrify orris <u>gentisin</u> lone
lapidate lusty lade

crescendo crimson violin mane
encyst lofty born
jacamar jaunty <u>vaginate</u> cane
mandolin mazy morn

Deborah Scott

Three Ships

I have three ships sailing the Sea of Life,
each having much to do with my destiny; but,
My Ship of Love has anchored in the
Harbor of Illusion.
My Ship of Freedom has run aground on the
Shore of Captivity.
My Ship of Ambition is sailing the Sea
of Hope on the Winds of Maybe
toward the Isle of Success.
And I, as fleet admiral in restlessness, count all the
desires of my heart and mind and use them as
sextants to navigate my ships onward to the
Continent of Happiness.

Deborah Scott

Loving In Silence

If you love me
Long in silence
I'll bake
You a cake
From the love
We make
And I'll savor it
With your tongue
And sing
You the song
Your silence sung

Stock Photo

Faces Moved by Different Pangs

1. Death of Loved One

Sadness oozes from under tattered joyous mask
coating face skin with sorrow enough
to make mountains cry
tooth enamel wilt.

Sour medicine, indescribable,
sinks into hearts like cadmium,
foul in taste and texture,
prolonging grief beyond reason.

Mortification becomes the new
mask worn before that unwanted
neighbor of all humans.

Face skin grimaces with the
notion that nasty mass will not
leave but morph into a hospitable
desire for termination.

Stock Photo

2. Rejection

Frowns constrict blood vessels so tight
skull aches like it's been ball-peened
(peening head) or nuked (caliber yield)
eyelids sag over pinpointed pupils
blood-shot eyes behind.

Sufferings stemming from the evil
in Man's soul, so sour it suggests
Heaven is not welcoming.

Pain of consistent denial
promotes a torture, a horror—
face skin contorts, resorts to
permanent wrinkles, furrows, messy folds.

Stock Photo

3. Unrequited Love

Faces at first smile at the thought
of loving to love, expecting love
to lure them into unknown
arms, unknown warmth, familiar bacteria.

Unreciprocated desire questions logic.
Lips, teeth, and jaws quiver
knowing warmth will not be shared.
Eyes drain with sinuses as indifference returns,
churning cheery hearts cynical.

Empty dead flesh droops from hollow bones like
Hollywood alien zombies
scary enough to move the moon
back a thousand miles
turn snakes to stone.

Stock Photo

4. Lost Love

Unexplained, unprovoked
no discussion, no second chance—
cursed, gone, over, left, done, no more.

Sickness crawls across faces
sticks like pus on public mirrors
hurts from rocket words
lodged in long-broken hearts
producing recurrent detonations.

when i was lonely and in boston

when i was lonely and in boston
i rode long on the mta
watched the morning people
squint in the brightness of day
watched children in the commons
and heard the bird's melody
swapping words for chirps
as thoughts of you inspired me

music was my purpose in boston
maybe it was an imperfect plan
fifteen minutes before the pops
plus a shake of mr fiedler's hand
the band made me feel welcomed
i played like God's gift was true
but with every pause, every breath
my thoughts returned to you

walking down huntington avenue
wanting in your warmth to hide
monophonic midday music
became my invisible guide
i sang your name aloud once
before a red light changed
the couple standing next to me
must have judged me deranged

the pops rejection was not harsh
no cause to be in rage
it was not that i didn't cut it
just charged to my youthful age
feeling misty i rounded a dark corner
the color of your coffee hair
as a tear fell from my left eye
all i could do was stare

feeling stupid, alone in boston
wishing for your kiss and hand again
there will be other ops i know
but why don't i feel better then?
tonight i love you while boston slumbers
and new jersey stars watch you sleep
i pray that safety be forever with you
and the hope you have for us will keep

Rejoice

    Conviction

        Asymmetric

Peeling

I'm being peeled like an orange:
Old stuff that would otherwise rot
in my mind causing stinking thinking.

A soft voice whispers, "Go through it."

I've been fighting and a couple of times
I went down fast
Face first on the mat.
I took punches that surprised me and
My opponent exploited every blow.

Robin Farrin

But strength is in my corner
My Lord is there with refreshments
that helps me to stand.
My opponent dances away
when I rise off the stool.
My skin is covered with divine, thick armor.

Four stars adorn my epaulettes, right shoulder and left shoulder:
Courage, strength, integrity, and truthfulness.
Their brilliance blinds my enemy.
He is not defeated but he flees the ring
And my tent stretches farther.

Morija Harris

There are songs and music in my heart
That I will write and sing and share.
This is a new thing being done to me.
This is a good thing being done in me.

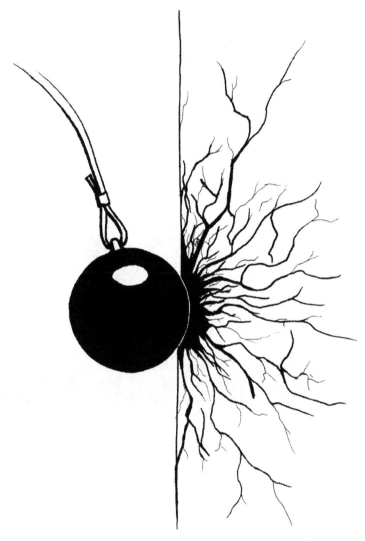

Deborah Scott

Wrecking Ball

Heal my hurts with joy
Your laughter knocks down old walls
I resolve to love.

Life Today, Not Tomorrow

Life to me:
sippin' licorice root tea,
fallin' snow masks imperfections in the yard,
playin' cards
Mannheim Steamroller airin' through the Bose
Jack Frost nowhere near my nose.

Childish laughter sets the mood:
no voices loud or rude.
Lazy noon makes all the difference today.
Come what may.
An unexpected call from my niece,
nothin's gonna snatch away my peace.

Invasion

One heart penetrant:
Seventeen touches per day.
Sunlight beams envy.

Jef Harris

ROK[3]

Hot fried silkworm snack.
Full moon shines in broad places.
Could this place be home?

---

[3] Republic of Korea aka South Korea

Morija Harris

Chicago Calling

Dreams of places and faces
Like Skokie and Wilmette,
Evanston and Northwestern U.
Chicago calling me out of the blue.

Blues bands jamming; White Sox slamming.
Stockyard stinking pig ears
Filling my empty stomach too.
Chicago calling me out of the blue.

Thoughts of games and names
Like Slot Cars and Al, Football and James
Donald and G-Men, then riots and fires.
Rusty nails piercing my foot through my shoe.
Chicago calling me out of the blue.

Love for a place shouldn't occupy so much space
In my Christ-centered heart and mind or should it?
Would it be a sin to smile and grin when
I think of the years spent braving that wind?

Chi Town is my town like Ronald's a McDonald's Clown
And life began downtown and in Old Town
Where Second City was found, then south in Hyde Park too.
Ah, Chicago calling me out of the blue.

O, windy City, dirty and pretty I still pray for you;
For Jerusalem, Bel Air, Hasborn, and New York too.
And heaven has a plan to heal your land.
Sweet home Chicago, you're missing your home too.
Chicago calling me: keep calling me out of the blue.

Wisdom

Lusty sights and sound
Luring quick curious peeks.
Trespasses subdued.

Unknown

Idle

Viscous hour hand:
Limited activity,
Rapid-fire mind.

Jef Harris

Blocked

The bridge to creativity is closed,
    letting in a non-permissive inspirational environment.
I can't create here.
    I labor at writing something right.
Something meaningful; a spark to ignite a flame;
    a bubble of impassible gas.
Conviction.
Here, words come but fall away hard and
    fast like Skittles on parquet floor,
bouncing once or twice then disappearing
    beneath double oven.
Two door refrigerator.
    It'll be years before that sweet morsel is seen again.

Color faded, sweetness tainted, maybe.
    A theme flashes.
A match idea in a dark room
        then vanishes with the smoke
from the burnt stem fast on a breeze
            that materialized just to whisk it away, then fades.
Too many things get lost around here.
        Not necessarily important things
but consequential nonetheless.
        It's loud, too loud.
Not words, just noise:
        Lopsided, syncopated, mumble jumble.
Not even the enlightening language of angels.
        Soapy distractions.
The lives of the many that don't bring inspiration.
        That don't encourage.
Not people anymore.
        Not since that one: that juvenile manuscript
with all the blank pages.
        I wonder who wrote that story up till now.
Who conspired? Collaborated?
        What experiences filled those pages with life?
People no more, forbid them seventh heaven!
        I draw from the wells of peace, quiet, and beauty.
Not here.

My Fall Thingy

Yeah, yeah, it's September school days cool days
I remember amber days are ahead I dread
the coming cold days and these old ways
but love the color
catapulting leaves once green
leaves and stems and hems fall in fall

Yeah, yeah fall thingy without definite
definition devoid of distinction
belittles the season for serious reasons
reduces significance makes it trite not right
but not out of sight dare I disdain
come what may except pain
yes, yeah, aye sans douleur[4] to be sure
heart pain unhealed wounds
pounds this season into being not seeing
I am not yet ready I regret being steady
enough to endure the manure

yeah I know I know the harvest, harvest time
harvest festivals harvest parties strawberries
corn apples squash pumpkins I spy a pie
about to be baked and yes, okay there's thanksgiving
I am giving thanks I give thanks in winter spring and summer
Bummer stupid hummer why isn't that enough for this
fall thingy stringing out three months
I'm not ready to fall prey to it again it's sin
I pray it's cut short like an Ork that ugly
demon thing that makes me sing the blues
and lose cues amid Fall hues and unkind clues
and overdue association dues and agonizing tools and rules

---

[4]   Without pain

Yeah, yeah back to school golden rule
bumblebee buses blocking boulevards bustling
Bored children to boring classes bored teachers and boring
subjects
(Hey fiddly dee we all got ADD! Hey diddle dee we all love
ADHD!)
Mine too to EDU and homeroom stew and homework due
For EDU and mean girls evil girls angry little wounded girls
And borderline boys too brawny for brains strain to
Regain maintain impossibilities individuality invisibility to
Sustain survival in this fall thing

Paraprosdokian
Credentials
Oblique

Her Mouth is Crooked

Her mouth is crooked.
       No visible scars.
            Her eyes dance;
mimics brilliant stars.

Her mouth is crooked.
       Once a broken jaw?
            Her bite is off.
To her a minor flaw?

Her mouth is crooked.
       Full pink lips,
            tidy white teeth.
She sings for more than tips,

in her red gown,
       in Seoul's south
            a worthy Hymn
with her crooked mouth.

Deborah Scott

10/07/07

A soft piano;
D Major lulling the soul.
Organs sing in tune.

Creativity:
Offspring of joy and quiet.
Take it back again.

Gifts and surprises
Suddenly appear in mail
Heaven sent no doubt.

O, I love to dance.
Smooth jazz, reggae, or the blues.
Legs, feet, knees, last long.

Jef Harris

Running After Men

I'm tired of running after men nurturing lopsided friendships.
Men, who never initiate, invite, invest or encourage.

I'm weary from running after men armed with just enough unction
to make me think that the friend they could be is real, when it's
pretend.
Men ready to take all that they need but give nothing in return.

I'm tired a chasing high-value targets who prove to be not worth
the dust on their shoes or under their shoes in the crevasses of
their soles.

I'm sick from running after men who don't understand what it
means to be a friend.
Perhaps once fired from friendships for lack of performance; men
who either think
too little of the concept or too little of the precept. Never
balanced, confident, or sure.

I'm through running after men who say they'll do one thing and
never do; men who repeat excuses liberally and rarely commit to
anything worthwhile.
Men with burly voices and curly secrets.

I'm tired of seeking men who need one true friend but
Can't get pass my skin to be one to me or trust the God in me
with their matters of the heart.

I'm dizzy from running after men who talk big, think little, talk
the walk but don't walk the talk; men too scared to dare to dream
but laugh at mine;
men who declare, direct, and dictate as they discourage.

I'm running from now on. Catch me if you can, man. Catch me if
you can.

Brown Boys

Brown boys brown boys
Lookin' 'round the streets for names
Brown boys brown boys
Castin' all their lots and guts in dangerous games
Brown boys brown boys
Livin' off the deathly power of lies
Brown boys ain't got no alibis.

Castin' blame on genes
Squanderin' teens
Stumblin' into toxic scenes
       That welcome with a gliss.
Claim a square on a road
Then flip off the justice code
What a flaky coping mode
       That vanishes with a hiss.

Brown boys brown boys
Wonderin' how you gonna stay alive?
Brown boys brown boys
How we gonna get revived?
Brown boys brown boys
Let's get our hearts aligned again,
Brown boys, to befall men.

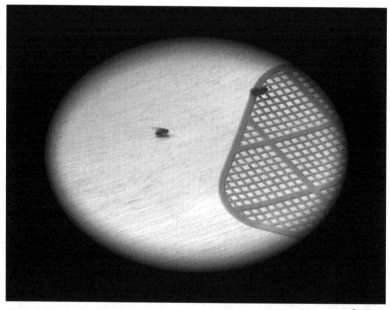

Jef Harris

Fly

With
your brother's
dried guts sticking
in square holes,
you dare harass me
with swatter in hand?
Your death
will be the zenith of my day!
For buzzing around
my ears and puking
on my Cannoli,
you deserve devastation,
splat!

Tennis

In Seoul, old warrior's
Backhand lobs soft bouncing balls
Amid patriarchs.

Veggies

Shiitake mushrooms,
Laura leeks, canola oil;
Vegan meal tonight.

Yellow Dust

Brown goo crust in eyes
An amber snow falls heavy.
It's yellow outside.

Jef Harris

A Chaplain Is Praying

A Chaplain is praying but a song surges in my heart.
    I can barely contain it.
My eyes open from reverence to see if anyone is looking at me.
    The sound escaped, or so I thought.
It was loud in me.
    The Chaplain is still praying.
I can't hear him: the AC unit overhead is too loud too.
    I hope his prayer avails much in heaven and
is effective in the hearts that can hear it, but his mic isn't.
    I'm going back to worship.
I want to sing about holiness, faithfulness, freedom, justice, and Love:
    His banner over me.
Besides, I live in His grip.
    I've gone beyond the limit
of my concentration on the Chaplain's prayer.
    I'm on to something bigger, something intimate and personal.
    Not universal, but something that changes me.
The medium for true change, effective change—
    One heart at a time, the least common denominator.
Enough time assembling with other believers.
    Time to ditch these congregants and let
My Shepherd lay me down in a green pasture where still waters are.
    There I'll sing of His love. There I'll ask for sheep to feed.
Show me someone to encourage and bless in whatever way You
    would have me to. Whatever way You would have me to.
Open my supernatural eyes, watch me move, and record my action.

Treats

Dancing on the roof
Beneath a pale crescent moon,
Chocolate on our mouths.

Nine Songs

Morija Harris

In this House

In this house . . . drama
Revolves spontaneously.
Crazy conclusions.

In this house . . . passion
With two midnight portions served.
Stomachs growl at dawn.

In this house . . . mail call
Shouts from multimedia,
No time to peruse.

In this house . . . vision
Backwards planning perfect sense,
Opportunity.

Lead Me

through darkness that surrounds me evil coaxing my hostility
temptations overwhelming borderline hatred in my heart
far beyond laughing demons dangling my desires from a string
they want to take my soul away they promise everything
as their loathing feeds me lead me lead me

pass the ignorance that delays me trust that now betrays me
pain of realizing all these faces aren't of prophets
mere devils masked so saintly flashing hope before my eyes
I'm lured to accept their passion apt to believe their lies
as their steel will bleeds me lead me lead me

up life-long loose rotting rungs pass this life's song poorly sung
over abysmal ridge move my feet my mind with surety
move my heart to love stand me again on blissful plains
I give to You my body my soul I give to You my reins
as my faith proceeds me lead me lead me

into a righteous state out of this shell of hate
safely into Your garden lead me
whole with Your sanctity circling inside of me
lead me lead me home

Ikengitmicelfout

Here I am this mornin' at three forty two.
Strummin' my guitar and thinkin' of you.
Wondrin' where you are and if you're all right.
Wishin' you could have danced with me all night.

My head's been full of music these past several weeks.
My fingers bend the strings I sing between the squeaks.
I'm believin' that this is where I belong:
Pourin' out my feelin's for you in a song.

G.E.M.'s been wondrin' why I stopped comin' round.
Whatever was between us hardly left ground.
We made no obligations no commitments were vowed.
No promises were spoken, at least not aloud.

I thought that Pistol Pete knew that I had it bad,
but a couple of times he made me mad
by teasin' me about the way I feel for you
and tellin' me I'm crazy when I'm bein' true blue.

I'm crankin' out some sounds that are new to my ears
and I'm thinkin' this is all gonna bring me to tears.
I don't care if it will I won't care if it don't
I won't care when it does and I don't care if it won't.

I know I shoulda told you that you swim in my veins,
but I thought that you would think I ain't got any brains.
And now that you know I know that you don't care
'Cause you'll be ETSin'[5] and I ain't goin' nowhere!

Yes I know I shoulda told you you're in charge of my dreams
And I know I shoulda told you a billion other things
It's too late for us now and I ain't gonna pout
If I could sing this song ikengitmicelfout!

Of wantin' you and hauntin' you to be what I need
Of shakin' and of achin' for your promise and creed
Of moanin' and of groanin' for the warmth of your kiss
Of breakin' and of achin' to be finish with this!

Ikengitmicelfout! Ikengitmicelfout! Ikengitmicelfout!
Ikengitmicelfout! Ikengitmicelfout! Ikengitmicelfout!
Ikengitmicelfout! Ikengitmicelfout! Gitmicelfout! Gitmicelfout!

---

[5]   Military initials meaning, "Earliest time of separation" or "separating",
        from the Army.

Satisfied

I've been out against the wind
I tried to catch it and it almost did me in
When times hung heavy like a gravestone 'round my neck
You cushioned every fall
And lifted me up Your tower wall.
And I'm smiling can't you see?
Though I've stumbled and I've cried
I know in whom I trust and my heart is warm
And I'm satisfied.

I've been wild but now I'm tame
I tried to beat the world at its own ruinous game
It left me weak and numb without the will to cope
But my strength will come again
And that will bring me gladness then
And I'm laughing can't you see?
Though my patience has been tried
I still know who I am and my mind is sound
And I'm satisfied.

And I'm dancing can't you see
Though I've wander and I've died
I'm Yours and Yours alone
And my spirit loves and I'm satisfied.

Eve

Mother of all human beings
Formed from a bone
Woman, forever bear your name.

> Listened to the Liar
> Now you bear in pain
> Forgiven, but you're still profaned.
> Eve, Eve. Look at what you've done to me.
> Eve, Eve. Mother what are you doing to me?

Yours is not all the blame
That man was with you
Adam, how'd you get to be you?

> With a sweaty face I eat my bread,
> Toiling everyday.
> Brooding a fake endurance here as dust.
> Eve, Eve. Look at what you've done to me.
> Eve, Eve. Mother what are you doing to me?

From the Garden whence you came,
Does Asia mimic you?
Africa? How can anyone imagine you?

> All of nature moans with you
> Especially me: Man
> Nonetheless, I'm grateful for your seed.
> Eve, Eve. Look at what you've done to me.
> Eve, Eve. Mother what are you doing to me?

Jef Harris

The Holes in the Rain

Listen and I'll tell you why I'm sitting here
Picking out the holes in a hard rain
I believed the war just wouldn't change my mind
I believed I really could stay sane.
One rainy night lightning flashed way out on the Gulf
A bomber left the shore above my head
Someone yelled up from the bottom of the tower
"We just heard that Harris was dead!"
I said, "We believed in music and in poetry
And in killing for survival and security."
Then I realized that he was talking about me.
Then he realized that he was talking to me.

Chaos and confusion abounds.
Chaos and confusion abounds.
Crazy: counting holes in the rain.
Crazy: counting holes in the rain.

I had opium for pain but nothing for the shock
Of seeing the smoking body of a fried man.
My Siamese sister sang a song of dying young
While walking on my back that night in Thailand.
She sang, "I believe someday my song will set me free."
I thought, "I believe the poppy'd do the same for me."
Then I saw myself a POW escapee
But they caught me and they hung me from a rubber tree.

Crazy: counting holes in the rain.
Crazy: counting holes in the rain.
Ataraxia.
Ataraxia.

Jef Harris

Flying through the clouds the next day pleased me some
But nothing could erase the smell of dead men
Or the memory of that brave young Siamese girl
A beauty in the heart of a great sin
Struggling for survival, praying hard for peace
But none will come as long as man's alive
I was looking for Utopia in the core of hell
Thought I found it up in bungalow five
Where she said, "What do you believe is really worth killing for"?
I asked, "What do you believe is really worth dying for"?

Where in the world is Heaven?
Where in the world is Heaven?
Crazy: counting holes in the rain.
Crazy: counting holes in the rain.

I asked myself these questions some sixty times that night
Before another thought came to my mind
If human life is balanced on an equal plane with death,
Is war the tool that keeps them both aligned?
I said, "Freedom is a cause I'm willing to kill someone for."
She said, "Freedom is a cause I'm willing to die for".

To be free is worth everything to me.
To be free in life and love is worth everything me.
To be free is worth everything to me.
To be free to hope in faith is worth everything me."

Ataraxia.
Ataraxia.

And so there I have told you why I'm sitting here
Picking out the holes in a hard rain.
Counting them before the splashes cover up
Evidence of the holes in the rain.
Evidence of the holes in the rain.

Fruit

I am not a gardener or a farmer.
When I whack weeds, everything goes
that doesn't have a flower.
When I water plants I drown them.
No, I'm not a farmer
And I don't know flowers.
>But I know fruit when I see it.
>I know fruit when I bear it:
>Fruit that restrains. Fruit that remains.

My passion is in pious pods;
Holy hormones to be shared
To be given away.
From birth till death
The harvest is not mine:
conspires to attract blessing.
>Yes I know fruit when I see it.
>I know fruit when I bear it:
>Fruit that restrains. Fruit that remains.

Fruit in my character.
Fruit in my conduct.
Fruit in my offspring.
Fruit in my words.
Fruit in my work.
Fruit that restrains. Fruit that remains.

Let the fruit of my lips
Be blessings stead curses;
holy kisses stead those of death.
Bad fruit won't possess me
As my heart bows before
the Beloved of Heaven.
>'Cause I know fruit when I see it.
>I see fruit when you bear it:
>Fruit that restrains. Fruit that remains.
>Good fruit good fruit good fruit and the bad.

Stock Photo

Outside

No, I don't know why she's in a shell
Nor how deep her pain roots inside
But I can tell she's miserable by what she shows outside

Outside her face frowned tightly
She walked as snow fell on her
She walked into the darkness that she shunned before

Outside no glow was present
Her eyes were dark and hollow
A loveless life can leave such awful scars

Outside the wind whipped pass her
The coldness froze within her
I said, "Hello!" But she just walked on by. Yes, she just walked on by.

    If I could just crack the crust that surrounds her then I
    Could penetrate deep inside of her world and I'm
    Convinced I would find a love as warm as God's

    But she's been hurt too many times and I just can't reach her
    She knew me before this change took her over
    But now like everyone else I'm stuck here outside her world.

Outside her world.
Outside her heart.
Now she's just one more broken-hearted bitter woman.
One more broken-hearted bitter woman becoming a weak man.

Screaming in ein Kissen[6]

I'm obsessed with seventh heaven
I have allies on seven continents
Some of them are fighters, some watchers
Some of them mediate and some bore tunnels
And cause rocks to roll away,
while some are held at bay.

Japan is in a horrible fix
While Washington is fighting in DC
And thinking of closing shop
In the middle of two wars and a NATO mixer
And North Africa is bounding out of ruts,
Moving with muscle and guts.

>On a white horse, coming soon I hope
>One day soon I'll be missin'
>Meanwhile I'll be on my knees
>Und screaming in ein Kissen.

Jerusalem is armed for Jihad
And financed to boot
The Old Testament and the New
Foretold and enlightens us of times
like these: grounds shake, oceans rise,
hearts break, minds shake, liars arise.

---

6 German for "Screaming in a pillow."

I'm aware that existential
Threats are prehistoric
But today they breed like locusts
And swarm in all the soft spots
Where resources are easy to take
And wills are easy to break.

> With eyes like fire, coming soon I pray
> The Ole Serpent will be hissin'
> While I'm on my knees
> Und screaming in ein Kissen.

Stand firm allies. Hold on to your hearts.
We're not done yet. It's just the beginning of the end.

Orthorectify

Innovate

Plethora

Hurt Men

Brokenhearted men
Steadily steal women's souls
Until they are numb.

Ballerina

how magnificent the motion of her graceful form
like the time-lapse opening of a flower's face at dawn
like an amorous pen flirting with a cob in springtime
like a panther slinking slyly through tall sunburnt grass

how gaily and precisely she fouettes roundabout
to an air of an oboe, mandolin, and bassoon
a trio piano largo and the oboe sing its part
like a nightingale rejoicing when the stars are high and bright

how whimsically and craftily she entices our applause
our thundering ovation caught her sparkling center stage
praising her performance as though it was some kind of god
courtly luring hearty interest in the dance we call an art

For Christa

Smooth Ride

In the name of love
Meet her emotional needs
And enjoy the ride.

Kiss a Frog

Failure happens, so
It's okay to kiss a frog
With eyes wide open.

On Faith

Joy relies on faith:
A fervent expectancy
My life will be good.

Submission

Arms hang down by side
Standing upright, inside prone
White flag waving soul.

What next?

The coming decades
Extremist groupthink gushes
Persistent conflict.

Globalization
Advancing prosperity.
Unfair dole of wealth.

Expired Thinking

Some people
don't seem to know
what year it is in which
they live.

They eat last year's tuna
with last year's mayonnaise
and last year's news,
take aspirin tablets expired
four years ago.

This physical stuff
isn't half as bad as
their thinking.

They think old.

Not seasoned with aged
wisdom, but antiquated,
stagnant.

Like the dust
in the corner behind
the chair never moved
since set there

twelve Februarys ago.

Thirty years old
thinking thirteen year old thoughts
and expecting change.

How is that possible?
Isn't that the stuff
insanity's made of?

It's not a disorder if an
entire city thinks that way; it's the norm.

They got that way by choice,
most of them anyway,
the rest by disease and genetics.

I will never bow to anyone
who thinks a magnitude below me.
How will I know?
How do you know?
Listening.

If I ever develop that condition,
someone please lobotomize me.

I Used To Wear A Ring On Every Finger

Reminders. Accolades. Memorials.
"JH" was a HS graduation/birthday present, seventeenth I think,
to myself.
My HS class of '69 ring still fits its original finger.
      With its blue gem, it's the favorite,
       second to my Turkish engagement ring.
That's the only one that fits my thumb and middle finger.
Its symbolism is more reflective than the others:
Acceptance. Origination. Significance.
My Jesus ring is a small ornate pinky ring.
Perhaps too gaudy for a man, but most essential;
      it reminds me of the power
      of the cross. With its cross within a cross,
It represents my crucifixion with the Christ.
The Thai puzzle ring has always been an
      icebreaker at mixers and a conversation piece.
          It was sold to me as white gold in the seventies
            but morphed to silver since then.
What did I know at nineteen about metallurgy?
Nichts. Nada. Nothing. Zilch.
      Gullible? Green?

Jef Harris

The rest are mediocre and not worth mentioning.
Each one was silver, except the wedding rings.
The first one was silver and gold:
          the lawn mower ate it and scattered its scrap
                    over thick fescue.
The sound was horrible realizing what it was.
The other one, given as a set by my mother-in-law,
was left on top of my Dodge's radiator.
          Distracted. Forgot. Closed the hood and drove off.
          The first bump or turn casted it away in silence.
My left thumb felt a bare finger.
That was when I stopped wearing rings.
But after playing a bejeweled Wise Man in a Christmas skit,
I would like to begin wearing rings again, I think.

Hope

I pledge allegiance
To admirers of hope
Who fail to give up.

Jef Harris

Jef Harris

3/11/08 (D Challenge)

Do a David dance
Down to drawers—double dare bare
Decisive dancer.

Overcome

    Somersault

        Mensuration

Absence

Slow dancing alone.
Chimes of freedom fade silent.
Crewless sloop slips by.

Behind

Behind schedule
Zigzagging through dark tunnels;
The end is not near.

Jef Harris

12-11-07

The more light we see at the end
of a tunnel means we are getting
closer to the truth.

Uncanny

Please remove your probe
From my frontal lobe, because
You are scaring me!

Jef Harris

I Will Never Go To Paris Again In Winter

That's right,
        I will never go to Paris again in winter.
                French hearts chill with cold winds.
Bitterness bites viscously.
        Bites tourists at the core of their national character,
        especially Americans.
                Algerian guards at the Louvre crunch hard into
                American character.
Condescending tones, words, snarled lips, and flared nostrils.
Disdain, contempt, and envy
        extrude from a single bite,
                "Americane!"[7]
Eyes size you up and down and sideways.
        The exception: New Year's Eve on the Champs-Élysées.
        "Bon Année"![8] "Bon Année"!

---

[7]   American
[8]   Happy New Year!

Jef Harris

As lustful Algerian men circle the crowd, hunting soft white
    <u>cheeks</u> for cheap double pecks.
        "Bon Année"! "Bon Année"!
Bold ones even try to steal lips.
      "Back you hound"! "Back I say"! "Those are my lips"!
         "Back, you man-beast"! "Loin[9]"! "Loin avec vous[10]"!
Thank God the girls turn away or step back. Blah!
    I'll never go to Paris again in winter even if she calls,
        begging me to visit when she is <u>bedridden</u> sick.
I'll go to Luxembourg City instead and dance through The Grund
    in her dry cold air, in a New York minute,
        before I go to Paris again in winter.
Ah, but Paris in Spring and Summer is to die for.

---

[9]   Away!
[10]   Away with you!

Unknown

Protest

I never marched against anything. I never marched for anything.
Walked for breast cancer once.
That was fun: warm sun, clear sky, soft supported shoes, pleasant
company.
Marched in lots of parades strutting military glory; pomp
and Boy Scout merit; cute and Cub Scout charm.
Limped ten kilometers in a parade in Holland because I refused to
quit my team.
Stress-fracture and two-toenails-loose dedication.
My protests have been behind closed doors, away from crowds.
Witnessed crowds turn bulldog ugly like the 1968 Democratic
Convention.
Chicago never bled as much as then.
I give money and time, sometimes.
I'd rather be helping the wiz behind the curtain,
pulling levers, mopping spit, and sweat,
than on the Yellow Brick Road where the witches and the flying
monkeys roam.
Nevertheless, I suppose I am a formidable protestant regardless:
Luchariscostal![11]

---

[11]   A blend of Lutheran, Charismatic, and Pentecostal

Robin Farrin

Nobody's Fool

To be humorous
But devoid of foolishness:
Far steps from a clown.

Jef Harris

Kaiserslautern

came later in my career
whispering in my ear
like a soft wind, "come home."
Come back to your one true love, first love.
Of all the places and foreign faces
to move into love and move to love,
once again, out of sin.
It was super. Supernatural.
It was a soft wind that brushed
against my ear and spawned a tear
and a call to fall in love again
but not a love like before.
Not like it was back when
my love was a lukewarm love
and the storm was not born of Thee.
This love was hot. This love is hot.

Jef Harris

Reunion

In the soul of Seoul
The pain of division screams
Amid distant hope.

Thoughts about the cost
Echo from Seoul to D.C.
Someone lifts a purse.

It's Stealing

I set up a high-tech display in the lobby of an auditorium
at MIT in Boston one spring.

On the table I had a dish filled with assorted hard candies.
You know, giveaways. Freebies.

It wasn't all that fancy, I thought.
Just a glass bowl I picked up at a Goodwill Store.

While I was attending a plenary in the auditorium,
someone dumped the candy in a pile on the table and took the dish.

How desperate was that? Gutsy, selfish.
Envy hates that you have what it doesn't have.
Envy hates to see you enjoy the fruit of your labor.

I had a clip with a sticky foam back that attached to a monitor
for holding papers for data entry.

The thief even removed the residual sticky stuff as if what remained
On the foam wasn't enough.

How depraved and deprived. Unprofessional for a government office.
Besides, it was mine not the Feds.
Jealousy demands an equal portion. It either takes yours
or schemes to get what you have or the next best thing.
Then, it loves to strut it before you. Jealousy will always put it on
display.

People steal motivated by jealousy and envy mostly, necessity
sometimes.
Some people don't want or need the things they steal,
they just don't want someone else to have them.
They think they can sell them for money.
Mostly the stuff ends in landfills, rivers, pawnshops, and fires.

The ultimate was the breaking into of my Illinois-tagged rental in
midtown
Manhattan and taking my luggage from the hatch.

The only priceless article contained therein was my 1985-86 journal.
Those precious thoughts, ideas, poems and prayers, now
speechless, muzzled forever.
I could not remember a thing. I wrote to Sweden to get one back.

The act even stole away my desire to write. Stole it away for over
ten years.
I blamed New York and almost forgave her last November.
She still owes me dreams, lost thoughts, and an unbroken heart.
Should I forgive her debt or choke it out of her?

Jef Harris

3/9/10

In physical warfare
there is always collateral damage
when prosecuting enemy strongholds.
In spiritual warfare there is always
collateral damage when we do not
prosecute enemy strongholds.

For Dr. Ed Smith

Sortie

His sword laid her open.
What was unseen became visible:
Soul, body, and spirit. No blood.
Bone did not crack or break.
Marrow remained intact.
Spirit recognized the blade and worked with him.
Her mind peeled back like an onion.
Fleshy leaf laid bare, stem, base, and root
      exposed before his double-edged foil.
He began carving out the lies that kept her from budding.
Curing emotional scars caused by word rockets, fragmentation
bomblets, and unrestrained tongues.
Mission accomplished,
      he returns inside his citadel
      to rest and refresh
      before his next sortie.

Devolution
Anaglyphs
Methodology

Epilogue

I do love the many attributes of language. German is harsh, but it is exact and unbending. On the other hand, the dialects make this language sing, but they are not all intelligible or universal.

French is languid, lyrical but sophisticated. I developed my love affair with this language after listening to a lot of Jacques Brel and Charles Aznavour songs. Imagine hearing a young Vietnamese girl sing Jacques Brel's *Ne Me Quitte Pas* or *Jef*—hauntingly awesome!

Of course English is my mother's tongue. Korean is intriguing but it proved too difficult to learn, or to invest time to learn it. Given the many times I've visited the country since 2007, I should be a Level 2 speaker by now, but I have not even made it to rung number one . . . I'm still just looking up the ladder thinking, "my that's high."

Poetry is a language in its own right and to understand any language takes practice. I offer you a few suggestions to gain understanding and appreciation:

- Read each poem more than once. It may take two mental recitations to get your heading and my voice.

- Google the words you don't understand. You will be amazed at what you might find while mining the meaning of words. And you can have fun doing it without becoming an etymologist.

- Try not to read the poems like you would read a newspaper; poetry is written to be heard. Take your time.

- Lend attention to what the poem is saying. You may be used to the words and speed by the meaning of the poem. Practice reading the poems aloud. Hear how the words chop and roll and pierce the air; take note of their affect on your lips, tongue, and throat.

If you like etymology, I challenge you to investigate the three underlined words in the poem *I Will Never Go To Paris Again in Winter*. How old are they? What are their original languages? While you're at it, check out the three underlined words in *"first poem of words."*

Jef, December 2011

Unknown

About the Author

Jef Harris is an avid poet who began writing lyric poetry, in Chcago at age 10. Throughout the 1970s and 1980s, he gave impromptu readings wherever he went, backing himself up on acoustic guitar. In Germany, he'd walk into a piano bar, sit at a piano, play, and either sing or recite his poetry. He once said, "Each song begins with a poem or a prayer." His poetry has been published by The World of Poetry Press, 1982; The New York Poetry Foundation Anthology, 1986; The American Poetry Anthology, 1983 and 1986; and other publications during 1980s—1990s, in Germany and America. In the Army, Jef became a prolific technical writer, which resulted in the publication of several technical reports and maunals. After military retirement, his technical and business writing skills were in great demand and he spent nine years devoting his talent to those genres. However, in 2003, he pledged a return to poetic expression. To him, "poetry not only speaks from the soul but also from the spirit of a living God dwelling inside, who sometimes permits the soul to speak." Jef lives in Bel Air, MD with his wife Christa, two daughters, and dog Bud E.

Sources

Lead Me—First published Spring 1986, *The New York Poetry Foundation Anthology*. The best of all reviewed entrants for the year 1986.

You Killed the Beauty—First published Summer 1986, *The American Poetry Anthology*, Volume VI, Number 2, ISBN 0-88147-017-1, ISSN 0734-5135

Three Ships—First published Spring/Summer 1983, *The American Poetry Anthology*, Volume II, Number 1-2, ISBN 0-88147-004-x, ISSN 0734-5135

Loving In Silence—First published in *Our Twentieth Century's Greatest Poems* 1982 by World of Poetry Press, LoC 82-050849, ISBN 0-910147-00-0

In this House—First published, 2008, *In this House: If Walls Could Talk*, FPI Publishing, Havre De Grace and Performed by Jef + Christa Harris, on the CD *In this House: If Walls Could Talk*, 2008, DoveEagle Records, Bel Air

Index to First Lines

About the Book

This first book is a personal reflection of experiences, places, peoples, trials, and successes of the author. The goal is to inspire by sharing poignant thoughts, encourage by spreading ardent hope, and enlighten by being honest and forthright. The words in this glittering collection of poems and songs form one of the most naked self-exposures undertaken by a retired Soldier. Jef Harris reveals himself with vibrant literary invention. Speaking face-to-face to his readers, he paints a colorful tapestry of language that invites you to read or listen, appreciate and understand as you relate to the emotive messages in his voice.